POETRY

March 2016

FOUNDED IN 1912 BY HARRIET MONROE

VOLUME CCVII · NUMBER 6

CONTENTS

March 2016

POEMS

CARL PHILLIPS	549	*Stray* *Wild Is the Wind*
GRETCHEN MARQUETTE	552	*Painted Turtle* *Want*
DENISE BERGMAN	554	*Terrarium*
DANTE MICHEAUX	555	*Theologies for Korah*
CACONRAD	560	*Mars.1* *Mars.2*
LEAH UMANSKY	562	*The Ambassadors—Part 5*
FELIX BERNSTEIN	564	*C*
JAMES REIDEL	565	*Miley Cyrus or Manatee?*
REBECCA HAZELTON	566	*The Good in the Evil World*
TOM SLEIGH	567	*House of Fact, House of Ruin*
KWAME DAWES	576	*Horns*
ALEC FINLAY	578	*Billia Croo*
JOHN ASHBERY	581	*Late-ish* *People Behaving Badly a Concern* *Day Bump* *Mean Particles*

PINTURA : PALABRA

FRANCISCO ARAGÓN	587	Introduction
LORNA DEE CERVANTES	590	*Night Magic (Blue Jester)*
BLAS FALCONER	593	*Orphan* *Revolution*
JUAN FELIPE HERRERA	597	*Radiante (s)*

BRENDA CÁRDENAS   599   *Placa/Rollcall*
Our Lady of Sorrows

IYAWÓ   602   *Soneto de Silueta*
Why Being "On Fire" Is for
Everyone

VALERIE MARTÍNEZ   607   *Larry Levan (snake)*
Granite Weaving

MARIA MELENDEZ KELSON   612   *Weaving Granite*
A Chingona Plays Miss Dinah
Brand

TINO VILLANUEVA   617   *Field of Moving Colors Layered*

EDUARDO C. CORRAL   619   *Testament Scratched into a Water*
Station Barrel (Translation #11)

ORLANDO RICARDO MENES   623   *El Patio de Mi Casa*
Altar Boy

CARMEN GIMÉNEZ SMITH   627   *Decoy Gang War Victim*
Only a Shadow

LAURIE ANN GUERRERO   631   *Brownies of the Southwest:*
Troop 704
Last Meal: Breakfast Tacos,
San Antonio, Tejas

COMMENT

CHRISTINA PUGH   639   On Ghosts and the Overplus

CONTRIBUTORS   646

Editor	DON SHARE
Art Director	FRED SASAKI
Managing Editor	SARAH DODSON
Assistant Editor	LINDSAY GARBUTT
Editorial Assistant	HOLLY AMOS
Consulting Editor	CHRISTINA PUGH
Design	ALEXANDER KNOWLTON

COVER ART BY JEFF ZIMMERMANN
"*Love Knot,*" 2015

POETRYMAGAZINE.ORG

A PUBLICATION OF THE
POETRY FOUNDATION
PRINTED BY CADMUS PROFESSIONAL COMMUNICATIONS, US

Poetry · March 2016 · Volume 207 · Number 6

Poetry (ISSN: 0032-2032) *is published monthly, except bimonthly July/August, by the Poetry Foundation. Address editorial correspondence to 61 W. Superior St., Chicago, IL 60654. Individual subscription rates: $35.00 per year domestic; $47.00 per year foreign. Library/institutional subscription rates: $38.00 per year domestic; $50.00 per year foreign. Single copies $3.75, plus $1.75 postage, for current issue; $4.25, plus $1.75 postage, for back issues. Address new subscriptions, renewals, and related correspondence to* Poetry, PO Box 421141, Palm Coast, FL 32142-1141 or call 800.327.6976. Periodicals postage paid at Chicago, IL, and additional mailing offices. POSTMASTER: Send address changes to Poetry, PO Box 421141, Palm Coast, FL 32142-1141. All rights reserved. Copyright © 2016 by the Poetry Foundation. Double issues cover two months but bear only one number. Volumes that include double issues comprise numbers 1 through 5. Please visit poetryfoundation.org/poetrymagazine/submissions for submission guidelines and to access the magazine's online submission system. Available in braille from the National Library Service for the Blind and Physically Handicapped. Available on microfilm and microfiche through National Archive Publishing Company, Ann Arbor, MI. Digital archive available at JSTOR.org. Distributed to bookstores by Ingram Periodicals, Media Solutions, Ubiquity Distributors, Small Changes, and Central Books in the UK.*

POEMS

CARL PHILLIPS

Stray

When he speaks of deserved and undeserved as more
than terms — how they can matter, suddenly — I can tell
he believes it. Sometimes a thing can seem star-like
when it's just a star, stripped of whatever small form of joy
likeness equals. Sometimes the thought that I'm doomed
to fail — that the body is — keeps me almost steady, if
steadiness is what a gift for a while brings — feathers, burst-
at-last pods of milkweed, October — before it all fades away.
Before the drugs and the loud music, before tears and
restraining orders and the eventual *go fuck yourself get your
ass out of here don't go*, the apartments across the street
were a boys' grammar school — before that, a convent,
the only remains of which, ornamenting the far parking lot,
is a marble pedestal with some Latin on it that translates as
Heart of Jesus, have mercy, as if that much, at least, still
remained relevant, or should. If it's true that secrets resist
always the act of telling, how come secrets, more often than
not, seem the entire story? Caladium, Cleome — how delicate,
this holding of certain words in the mouth, the all but lost
trick of lifting for salvage the last windfalls as, across them,
the bees make their slow-muscled, stunned, moving scab...

Wild Is the Wind

About what's past, *Hold on when you can*, I used to say,
And when you can't, let go, as if memory were one of those
mechanical bulls, easily dismountable, should the ride
turn rough. I lived, in those days, at the forest's edge —
metaphorically, so it can sometimes seem now, though
the forest was real, as my life beside it was. I spent
much of my time listening to the sounds of random, un-
knowable things dropping or being dropped from, variously,
a middling height or a great one until, by winter, it was
just the snow falling, each time like a new, unnecessary
taxonomy or syntax for how to parse what's plain, snow
from which the occasional lost hunter would emerge
every few or so seasons, and — just once — a runaway child
whom I gave some money to and told no one about,

having promised ... *You must keep what you've promised
very close to your heart, that way you'll never forget*
is what I've always been told. I've been told quite
a lot of things. They hover — some more unbidden than
others — in that part of the mind where mistakes and torn
wishes echo as in a room that's been newly cathedraled,
so that the echo surprises, though lately it's less the echo
itself that can still most surprise me about memory —
it's more the time it takes, going away: a mouth opening
to say *I love sex with you too it doesn't mean I wanna stop
my life for it*, for example; or just a voice, mouthless,
asking *Since when does the indifference of the body's
stance when we're alone, unwatched, in late light, amount*

to cruelty? For the metaphysical poets, the problem
with weeping for what's been lost is that tears
wash out memory and, by extension, what we'd hoped
to remember. If I refuse, increasingly, to explain, isn't
explanation, at the end of the day, what the sturdier
truths most resist? It's been my experience that

tears are useless against all the rest of it that, if I
could, I'd forget. That I keep wanting to stay should
count at least for something. I'm not done with you yet.

Painted Turtle

Summer road the ring around the lake, we drove mostly in silence.

Why aren't I your wife?

You swerved around a turtle sunning itself.

I wanted to go back. To hold the hot disc of it and place it in the grass.

We were late for dinner.

One twentieth of a mile an hour, I said. *Claws in tar*. You turned the car around.

Traffic from the direction of the turtle, and you saw before I did, the fifty bones of the carapace,

crushed roman dome, the surprise of red blood.

I couldn't help crying, couldn't keep anything from harm.

I'm sorry, you said, and let it hurt.

The relief, always, of you in the seat beside me, you'll never know.

Driving that road next winter, you remembered that place in the road. *Your turtle.*

During hibernation, a turtle's heart beats once for every ten minutes.

It cannot voluntarily open its eyes.

Want

When I was twelve, I wanted a macaw
        but they cost hundreds of dollars.

If we win the lottery? I asked.
        Macaws weren't known to be great talkers,

but they were affectionate.
        Yes, my mother said. *If we win the lottery.*

I was satisfied, so long as it wasn't impossible.

The macaw would be blue.

DENISE BERGMAN

Terrarium

a netless somersault, the trapeze swing disappears in disheveled clouds among cumulus sheep, birds, rowboat

the feather on the Joseph Cornell narrow shelf, unruffled as the one we pocketed from the grass in a nearby park to share week by week her house mine but soon forgot and it sat on her dresser maybe sits there still

elsewhere, heat, light, a shut-eye bat hangs, a limp cyclamen stem straightens, an avocado ripens, a grapefruit tree in a winter kitchen leafs out of season. Wednesday is a calendar X, Thursday, Friday, the impulse: turn inward

start with near then far. narrow then broad. wayward then home-bound, that, too, is near then far, inward. rate the prospects 1 to 10, Yelp the day 1- to 4-star: accommodations, host, did it match the advertised expectation

the box on your lap, open it up. open your lap, open it up and your arms, a is for arm. b is for box, c connection, go on, break the seal, unfold the replacement net

DANTE MICHEAUX

Theologies for Korah

FROM LOCUSTS AND WILD HONEY

On a lesser diet than that of the wretched
rests a prophecy: some of us come to prepare.
I stood before my god, at a foreign altar,
and promised to guide you; me, with my heretic
theology. I practice the ways passed to me
by descendants of followers of a wild man:
followers in the desert downwind of his musk,
listening to him confess himself unfit to
loose latchets on shoes; they believed his words holy,
ignored bits of insect wing in his beard. And then,
he told them of a dove that no one else could see.
I have learned to retain my head while speaking truth.

Do I reject the glamor of evil? I do.
You are creation — the same after water and
after the Holy Spirit, only now you see
the door to life and unto the Kingdom of God.
Do not feel the need of any claimant to royal
priesthood. Some ancient, calling himself Peter, must
have been in his cups when he wrote that ish. The nerve!
You were cleansed with water by power of the Word.
Sign of the Cross? Phooey! There is no miracle
in an instrument of death. See: Martin Luther,
theses 5, 16, 28, and 95.
God made no symbols; people did, et cetera.

Not much older than you when she first saw the Christ
— seated in glory with few of His disciples —
who gave her many gifts: a consummate marriage
by way of His foreskin; the blesséd stigmata;
and her head as a bag of rose petals. To "build
a cell inside your mind," a cell of self-knowledge,
is good advice, my child. The Christ commanded her
to open the eye of her intellect and gaze
into Him. This made her secularly gifted,
a power broker. Read her correspondence, yes,
the letters of a lunatic diplomat but
heeded, virtuous sweet amorous Word of God.

EPHPHATHA RITE

He sighed. All power in heaven and in earth is.
Be opened. Hear and speak the truth but tell no one
how. Superior to the purifications
of Old Law was that water. Be opened, daughter.
All power in heaven and earth is. No questions.
Be opened. Hold fast to my teachings, not those of
stewards but my words. Seek you first, girl, the kingdom
of my love, with all your mind. All your mind. Do not
forget your mind. You are mine. Be opened. Power!
Suffer it to be so now: for thus it becomes
us to fulfill all righteousness. All power in
heaven and in earth is given me. Be opened.

CODA PATRINALIS

In the land of mama there is a cathedral,
the cathedral of the Holy Spirit. Inside
is an icon, an image of Theotokos.
Once old enough to go solo, after an age
of discernment is reached, perhaps in passing by,
go there. Make your way up the nave and to the right;
there you will find her looking at you, babe in arm,
tired and anemic as usual. Bless her
with a kiss and make her holy. Bless the babe, too,
if feeling generous. Use a chair if needed.
It is a painting. Simple miracles were made
on a lesser diet than that of the wretched.

Mars.1

to be
gone a
constant desire
embarrassed for the
giant leaning in for love
we had enough
of
the dance number but   the whirling begins
it just starts
silos full of air
no more corn
no more wheat
watching myself for
full details in a strange man's pants
we let
the soldier board the plane
shot in head three days later
why are you angry you said
why are you not I said

Mars.2

to worship
tininess of a
martyr
observe
shrinking
church in
rearview
mirror
the black deer
it turns out was
beige a tan doe
covered in flies
flesh of shame
is nearly the
shame of flesh
pressing an unstable
clock to cactus with one,
two, three counts of recalibration
fuck you who ask for
forgiveness instead of
permission   all
clocks are precarious inscrutable windows

LEAH UMANSKY

The Ambassadors — Part 5

+

This is a poured-truth dressed in memory
and cut down; this is a matter ruff; a gray middle
the world is in flight and many things circle.

     What world do you want me in? I ask.

But I am confronted with touch, the work of hand and eye,
and a kept-remark roaming...
          When in Rome, I think.

+

A dressed-memory: never did more frill mean curtained-silence.

     Hello?
     We're here, they say.

I remember the moment first-harvested: no possible brimming is
ever frank. At that age, who knew filth could be forward. I thought
I could cut it down.

+

Look, the leaping is possible, I think. I watch the way evening attaches
to us. See its starting point? It banded, uncontrolled and gleaming.
Our jewel. Not all worlds see the darkness.
Remember: the world is good, that leaping center is a tuned heart.
I want that melody.

+

What world do you want me in, now? I ask
I feel broad-throated, and slippy.
I say, *tell me the times the chronicle mentions me.*

      56, she says.

Let me be clear: I knew. I said, I knew. I wanted to have my own grown romance.
      Plant me another. Do it now.

FELIX BERNSTEIN

C

metaphor waits at the
foot of his name

on thursday he'll
cancel experience

metaphor waits for
him to shovel the snow

on thursday he'll
crush experience

Miley Cyrus or Manatee?

What is flat and nothing but skin,
What lolls in a shallow world,
What is watched for its surface,
Between long episodes of water the color of a dead screen's
    sea-green glass,
What has but a few hairs in the snapshot?
A bit of muzzle,
No more than a pug's worth for a rented red kayak,
For this sailor swallowed by enormous wax lips,
What is gray and aporial,
Once mistaken for half girl,
Half monster,
Disappointingly naked and slipping under the hull.

—*Lido Beach, Fla., November 2013*

REBECCA HAZELTON

The Good in the Evil World

Before the war leaned in and blew out
the candles, there were many long days
where lovers called themselves lovers
and a house was a dream but also
four walls, a roof. A father called
to his daughter to see the monarch butterflies,
pausing in their migration to fan the goldenrod,
a tiger in each coy disclosure.
A young man reached for a blackberry
and found draped on a branch a green snake
the color of matcha. A snake the color of matcha
sighed in the sun. People drove in cars.
There were jobs and someone had to work
every morning. A man quit his job
but it was no tragedy. He didn't like the work.
Another man slid in and found it comfortable
enough, and just as easily slid in beside
the man's wife and into the everyday rhythms
of his life and that was no tragedy either.
After rains, a ring of mushrooms would delicately
crack the earth. Spanish moss harbored red mites.
The sky wasn't interesting. No one looked up.

TOM SLEIGH

House of Fact, House of Ruin

I. HOMILIES FROM HOME

You've got to put your pants on in the house of fact.
And in the house of fact, when you take off your shirt,
you can hear your shirt cry out, *Facts are the floor, facts
are how you make the right side talk to the left.*

I'm washing my naked belly clean, and doing it with dignity.
I'm turning around, trying to see the filthiness
that keeps making me filthy. I've scraped away
my molecules right down to the atoms' emptiness

and arranged the map's folds so that nobody
can see it breaking into fits of weeping.
Now that even our eyes have their dedicated poverties,

now that even our eyes are chained to their slavish occupations,
whatever the soul lacks drains the soul to nothing.
I hate to admit it, but even the house of fact is a house of ruin.

2. REST

The strange is done with, over,
the strange that late at night you returned
to chat with again and again. No longer will anyone
wait for me in my corner where

good is bad, where that tight-lipped morning
of tears by the bay means nothing anymore
to anyone. To be cleared of the inks that stain
my ankles while watching my eyes go blind in the mirror

is the kind of rest that the seventh day promises
but never brings. Instead, the species
climbs aboard the ark of copulation

and ignores the forty days and nights of rain.
And the much-talked-of soul that the rain denies
burrows deep into the mud of so much pain.

3. SPIDER

Look at the spider with the enormous body and tiny head,
a spider of no color: today, when I kneel
down to look at it more closely, its many arms nailed
to a many-armed cross are a prayer in a code that only God,

who's forgotten it, can decipher. And its eyes
invisible to my eyes, which guided it like a pilot
through the wilderness of space,
no longer steer its legs across the intricate,

almost-not-thereness of its web. Each thread
it spins with the finality of fate divides its head
from its body. And the poor thing,

even with so many legs, doesn't know which way to run.
Just look at its abdomen, huge as the stone blocking
what's-his-name's tomb, that the head's condemned to drag around.

Honestly, when I look at life straight,
I'm just another blind Brooklynite — not because
I can't see that Jean-Jacques was an idiot,
or that Saint Peter being nailed to the cross

upside down isn't the purest measure
of my humanity, but because my eyes
can't see my illiterate skeleton and the razor
and cigar that will outlive me. So try to save a day

for when there are no days, reason with the lens
inside every healing wound, witness how your
own inner grace, gnawing at itself, gets baptized

in phosphates of hemlock and error.
And so what if the sunset arrives from Athens?
So what if no trace of anyone survives?

5. THE LAST TO BE EXCUSED

Remember the old aunts, sarcastic,
chain-smoking, gesturing with their canes,
scoring point after point with their widowed lungs?

How was I to eat with them as they pushed
around their plates not peas and carrots
but distance and disdain for their silly nephew

still trying, at his age, to forget
how being old is as new to the old
as being just born is to the just born —

even their glued-together, half-cracked
china radiates impatience for the pity
that the young want them to want.

The way they kept saying MOTHER —
like it was all in caps — saying it like that
as if they still felt her eyes on how

they handled their knives, forks, spoons,
making each bite harder to swallow.
The day is coming when there'll be no water

in the pitcher, no eternally dying father
served up like canned spinach and corn,
no brooches of affection their absent lips

pin to the air. And as that silence
slowly breaks the hours in two, I'll be
left alone to dine with the nothingness

that, just for form's sake, says grace.
The table will be set with shadows,
the phantom food served up by shadows —

and all the dead mothers come to this repast
will sit down on chairs of dust
in the wake of that last supper

in the kitchen gone cold where I'll hear the last
maternal "Serve yourself, Tom"
smothered by that dark where no one can tell

the knife blade from the handle,
or the food from the plate, or the plate
from the table, or if there's a table at all.

6. THE ETERNAL DICE

OMG, it makes me cry to admit that I am human;
to feel the heaviness of all your bread I've eaten.

Oh sure, you claimed you raised me from the dust,
but where's the wound fermenting in your side?

You know nothing of those Marias who split for good.
OMG, if you'd been born a human being

today you'd know how to behave like God.
But in your always everywhere hard partying with perfection

you feel nothing of the pain of your creation.
And so it's us, the poor fuckers who suffer, who must be god.

Today, in my middle-aged pupils, I see the glare of candles
lit for my death-row vigil. OMG, old gambler, take up

your crooked tricks again, and let's throw your cooked pair of dice —
in the fated luck you dole out to the universe

maybe we'll roll snake eyes staring back at us like death,
maybe you'll deal two aces black as the grave's mud.

OMG, in this night gone deaf and blind,
you won't be able to play because the poor Earth itself

is just a single die whose edges have grown rounded
by rolling too many eons through the battering sky

and nobody now can stop it until it rolls into a hole,
the vast hole, OMG, inside a single molecule.

7. THE OTHER GARDEN

In the Garden there was a spider.
And because the man knelt beside him, the spider
overheard him, the agony of his prayer
like the fear of a fly who can't steer

any other direction than into the web stretching out
no matter which way the fly veers. The spider
felt the threads of all being vibrate
through him — and so it vowed to be the answer

to the prayer of the man praying to his father
to let this cup pass. But on the cross, when the man cried out
to his father not to abandon him, his father

did abandon him. And so the spider
vowed to weave a web so tightly around the father that the harder
he'd struggle the more he'd be caught.

8. WHAT HASN'T YET COME IS ALREADY OVER

If it rains tonight, will a raindrop be my cell?
Will the bars the sky lets down
take one look at me and turn to steel?
Now that the hot afternoon is finally done,

done the cups of tea we drank with your mother,
I want to ask the rain to yank my strings
back a thousand years. But even back that far,
will the rain still be my prison?

To be lost in the minutiae
of our vacations from the soul, to forget
the Vedic threads spun out beyond my end,

to press against your breasts obedient
to the purest pulses. Yeah, sure. Make the story
of my life the story of my never having been.

Horns

In every crowd, there is the one
with horns, casually moving through
the bodies as if this is the living

room of a creature with horns,
a long cloak and the song of tongues
on the lips of the body. To see

the horns, one's heart rate must
reach one hundred and seventy
five beats per minute, at a rate

faster than the blink of an eye,
for the body with horns lives
in the space between the blink

and light — slow down the blink
and somewhere in the white space
between sight and sightlessness

is twilight, and in that place,
that gap, the stop-time, the horn-
headed creatures appear,

spinning, dancing, strolling
through the crowd; and in the
fever of revelation, you will

understand why the shaman
is filled with the hubris
of creation, why the healer

forgets herself and feels like
angels about to take flight.
My head throbs under

the mosquito mesh, the drums
do not stop through the night,
the one with horns feeds

me sour porridge and nuts
and sways, *Welcome, welcome*.

ALEC FINLAY

Billia Croo

culture is richest where there's
the greatest ratio
                        land : coast

                              — *After Barry Cunliffe*

•

this patch of the western
ocean's coruscating garden

recalls my favorite song
(mishearing) *the sea's very hum-*

drum ... — but no, there's not
one ocean, not when such an

infinite mix of blues can
outshine the map's cerulean

•

the sea is there for a solan
to push his wings against

or plunge in, reinventing
the medium — when the light

comes right through them
the waves let slip wrack

and tangle, pitching round
until they go breaking on

the boulder beach, crashing
under Row Head, hassling

brittlestars and urchins, or splash
near the shelducks dozing

on their green sun shelf—
there's no need to worry

that any wave is wasted
when there's all this motion

•

along the bay there's
the promise of a new world

from each new device connect-
ed to the cable that runs

out under the wild rocks,
into the diamond space

inside those three buoys—
this is where the metal

gets salt-wet: and that's
the only true test—the problem

is elastic: what kind of roots
will grip fast with moorings

subject to ebb, flood, flux,
in a surge of such force?

•

what's solid was once liquid
as with rock and sand

which nature divided —
like us — these waves were

tugged and formed, in
slowness, slowness that

we've lost, for there's no
way to relearn the tide's

happy knack of infinitesimal
growth, except by sloshing

around, or waiting, stranded,
on the heave of the moon

JOHN ASHBERY

Late-ish

The girl in the green ski chasuble
hasn't yet graduated from radio school.
Let's pay attention.

Looking ahead, why, he waved his mouth along.
Doesn't life get difficult in the summer?
The divine medicine for it collapsed
in front of the shortstop,
who took off like a battalion.

Crowds of older people who would read this
happily, willingly, then walking into night's embrace,
then kiss. *"To turn you out, to turn you out!"*
Sometimes an arm is accused:
You could have felt it, the blue shirts,
phlegm central, four times a night.
But what does that get me?
Light refreshments.

When the suburban demonstration kind of shrunk
you put your foot out,
leave it or kiss it
or even two years ago,
Charmaine here tells us.
I think I should stay …

Cross-eyed sonofabitch …
He liked him, he could tell. A de-happening.
The gangster no longer wanted to sleep with him,
but what the heck. With time off
for actual fuzz collected … All right, boys.
Cheap murders, peach driven … I seen enough of those
samples along the way.

People Behaving Badly a Concern

Aggressive panhandling, public urination, verbal threats,
public nudity and violation of the open container law
followed us down the days, for why
are we here much longer,
or even this long? I ask you
to be civil and not interrupt night's business.

It was fun getting used to you,
who couldn't have been more nicer.
This was as modern as it had ever been.
They were influenced by him: some dirty magazine
on the air tonight. (Amid the chaos, reports of survivors.)

Didn't the flowers' restoration cat fugue keep spilling,
and like that? It wouldn't be the first time, either.
The pro-taffeta get up and laugh,
investigate or communicate. The night you were
going to stay up late, others will kiss,
and he talks about you, and I don't know what.
Come in, anyway,
and don't lack for tales of the Assertion.

We're talking civilian unrest.
Yes, well, maybe you should take one.

(Do not bite or chew.)

Day Bump

Whether the harborline or the east shoreline
consummated it was nobody's biz until you got there,
eyelids ashimmer, content with one more dispensation
from blue above. And just like we were saying,
the people began to show some interest
in the mud-choked harbor. It could be summer again
for all anyone in our class knew.
Yeah, that's right. Bumped from our dog-perch,
we'd had to roil with the last of them.

It's taken a while since I've been here,
but I'm resolved. What, didn't I print,
little piles of notes, slopes almost Sicilian?
Here is my friend:
Socks for comfort (now boys) will see later. Did they come?
The inner grocery had to take three sets of clips away.
Speaking to him of intricate family affairs.
I'm not what you think. Stay preconscious.
It's just the "flooding of the council." No need to feel afraid.

Mean Particles

Sometimes something like a second
washes the base of this street.
The father and his two assistants
are given permission to go.
One of them, a woman, asks, "Why
did we come here in the first place,
to this citadel of dampness?"

Some days are worse than others,
even if we can't believe in them.
But that was never a concern of mine,
reasoned the patient.

Sing, scroll, or never be blasted by us
into marmoreal meaning, or the fist for it.
Kudos to the prince who journeyed here
to negotiate our release, if you can believe it.

You're right. The ballads are retreating
back into the atmosphere.
They won't be coming round again.
Make your peace.

PINTURA : PALABRA

Introduction

At the 2010 Latino Art Now! conference in Los Angeles it hit me — the nagging feeling that Latino artists and poets aren't meaningfully aware of one another, or of the canvases and poems that flourish in their respective fields. It left me wondering: How might we aspire to bridge this gap?

A year later, a potential opportunity emerged when I learned that the next Latino Art Now! would convene in Washington DC in the fall of 2013. The conference, which brings together scholars, historians, collectors, and artists, would intentionally coincide with the opening of *Our America: The Latino Presence in American Art*, a major exhibit featuring seventy-two artists, with artworks spanning from the fifties to the present. Guided by the vision of E. Carmen Ramos, curator of Latino art at the Smithsonian American Art Museum, sixty-three of the exhibit's ninety-two pieces were added to the permanent collection expressly for the show. Ramos would prove to be an instrumental advocate and ally for the project I had in mind.

"PINTURA : PALABRA, a project in ekphrasis" is a multi-year initiative overseen by Letras Latinas, the literary program of the University of Notre Dame's Institute for Latino Studies, and partially supported by the generosity of the Weissberg Foundation. A panel I moderated on poetry and art at the aforementioned DC conference served as the initiative's official launch in November 2013. Since then, the initiative has evolved into a range of related activities to encourage the creation of art-inspired poetry: curated workshops at the traveling exhibit's host museums; self-directed on-site residencies with the exhibit serving as a prompt; and invitations to selected writers to respond to the exhibit remotely, via its gorgeously produced catalog.

The principal "outcomes," if you will, have consisted of portfolios published in partnering journals. Two have appeared thus far in *Poet Lore* and *Notre Dame Review*. Another three are in the works and forthcoming in *The Los Angeles Review*, *The Packinghouse Review*, and *Western Humanities Review*. With twenty poems by twelve poets, this is the lone portfolio of the PINTURA : PALABRA initiative that includes reproductions of the artworks alongside the poems, thanks to the generosity of the Smithsonian American Art Museum.

In the pages that follow, readers will experience how rich and unpredictable Latino poetry can be. For example, the portfolio includes poems by three Chicano/a elders: Juan Felipe Herrera, Lorna Dee Cervantes, and Tino Villanueva. Anyone familiar with the history of Chicano poetry might consider those terms ("Chicano/a" and "elder") and expect a poem about, say, Frank Romero's *The Death of Rubén Salazar*. (One of the exhibit's major pieces, it is a large canvas that depicts an iconic and tragic moment during the National Chicano Moratorium march in Los Angeles in 1970.) Instead, our current US poet laureate riffs off of Olga Albizu's abstract work, *Radiante*, an image that graced, as did other color-rich Albizu images in the sixties, the covers of various jazz albums. Villanueva's poem, "Field of Moving Colors Layered," is a reflective monologue about Alberto Valdés's abstract *Untitled*. Cervantes, for her part, invokes Lorca's rhythms with her trance-inducing repetition of "blue" in her particular take on Carlos Almaraz's neo-expressionist work, *Night Magic (Blue Jester)*.

I highlight these poets and artworks to demonstrate that where one might expect a more explicitly political poetry, that expectation is thwarted. This is not to say there aren't any political works here — there certainly are — but Latino art and poetry are too often assumed to be exclusively political. The images presented in this portfolio showcase the variety of mediums and themes within modern and contemporary Latino art. Likewise, this selection of poems underscores multiplicity as a mirror of what Latino poetry is today.

Night Magic (Blue Jester), 1988, by Carlos Almaraz

LORNA DEE CERVANTES

Night Magic (Blue Jester)

After Federico García Lorca

Blue that I love you
Blue that I hate you
Fat blue in the face
Disgraced blue that I erase
You lone blue
Blue of an alien race
Strong blue eternally graced
Blue that I know you
Blue that I choose you
Crust blue
Chunky blue
Moon blue glows that despise
You — idolize you
Blue and the band disappears
Blue of the single left dog
Blue of the eminent red fog
Blue that I glue you to me
You again and again blue
Blue blue of the helium
Bubble of loveloss
Blue of the whirlwind
The blue being again
Blue of the endless rain
Blue that I paint you
Blue that I knew you
Blue of the blinking lights
Blue of the landing at full tilt
Blue of the wilt
Flower of nightfall
Blue of the shadow
In yellowed windows
Blue of the blown
And broken glass

Blue of the Blue Line
Underlines in blue
Blue of the ascending nude
Blue before the blackness
Of new blue of our winsome
Bedlam Blue of the blue
Bed alone: blue of the one
Who looks on blue of what
Remains of cement fall
Blue of the vague crescent
Ship sailing blue of the rainbow
Of wait blue that I whore
You — blue that I adore you
Blue of the bluest door
Blue my painted city
In blue (it blew.)

Nocturnal (Horizon Line), 2010, by Teresita Fernández

BLAS FALCONER

Orphan

I'd come to help settle your
mother's affairs. On the last night,

we ate where she worked all
her life. *Now that she's gone,*

you said, *I'll never come back.*
Looking out over the dark, you saw

a light in the distance, a boat
crossing the bay, and told

the story of the fisherman
cursed to float adrift

forever. You hadn't thought of it
since you were a child, and held

your hand across the table to
show me how it trembled.

I didn't understand until, alone,
years later, wandering the city where

I was born, I stood before
a black wall, polished to shimmer,

and it looked to me like the sea
at night, hard and endless.

Platanal, 1974, by Myrna Báez

Revolution

Considering Myrna Báez's painting Platanal, *E. Carmen Ramos explains,*
"When Puerto Rico was a Spanish colony, artists like Francisco Oller depicted the
plantain as both a key accoutrement to the jíbaro (rural peasant) and a metaphor
for the island's independent cultural identity."

Plantain trees gather at the edge
of the orchard, clamor for light

in the foreground. They seem to grow
as one, as if they'd fill the field

and the mountains behind them,
leaves large and frayed. We stood

there, once, or someplace like it, so
here we are again, it seems,

years later, branches leaning over
the road, you in your long skirt,

looking out as if to recall something
you meant to do. *My country*, I hear

you say still. But if that's dusk
in the hills, you know what's

coming to the field. You'll stand
among them till there's nothing left

to see. I'll wait beside you, though
I don't know what we're waiting for.

Radiante, 1967, by Olga Albizu

JUAN FELIPE HERRERA

Radiante (s)

Jestered ochre yellow my umber Rothko
divisions my Brooklyns with Jerry Stern
black then oranged gold leaf & tiny skulls
perforations Dada sugar bread of Oaxacan
ecstasy Lorca's green horse the daffodil head
corruptions of the State in tenor exhalation
saxophonics blossomings rouged monkey
Dalí roll down the keys the high G's
underStreets of the undeRealms my hair.

Throttle up into hyper-city correlations =
compassion compassion

the void extends

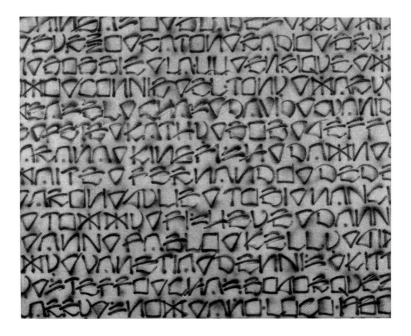

Placa/Rollcall, 1980, by Charles "Chaz" Bojórquez

Placa/Rollcall

If the city was a body, graffiti would tell us where it hurts.
— Charles "Chaz" Bojórquez

And this block would shout, "Nos diste un CHINGASO, cabrón. Mira esta cara rota, these baton-cracked ribs, this black and blue street dizzy con gente: BLADES, KIKI, LARRY, SNOW, ENRIQUE, CONNIE, ELTON, KING, DAVID, KELLY, JEFF, RATÓN, CHAZ, los de aquí, los de abajo. This roll call won't be silenced, not by glock, not by chokehold. This is our temple of runes, our tomb — its glyphic curve and flow, calligraphic code writ acrylic. This, our relic, our scroll unrolled in catacombs, our flecks of subtext still buzzing después de que vayamos con La Pelona. ¡QUÉ LUCHA, LOCO! Ven, baile con nosotros to the aerosol's maraca y hiss, al punk en español's furious sweat. Hang your head out the window y dale un grito tan lleno de duende that it cracks the pavement, summons our dead to dinner. Turn the tonal kaleidoscope. Then pause, catch your breath, so you don't miss the illegible moment where all the mystery lives. There, de-cypher *that*!"

Untitled, from the *Silueta* series, 1980, by Ana Mendieta

Our Lady of Sorrows

has appeared to the mountain
    dwellers, her grief engraved
where stone softens to clay. Keep
    your eyes sharp for a dagger.
In its hilt, you'll find her face
    pressed to the earth's cheek. Kiss
this sacred spot before the rains
    wash it away like her orphaned
feet. Notched heart cradles
    a planet heavy with night-
mares flying into empty mouths.
    Listen for their thirsty murmurs.
She'll push her ponderous child
    into the dew of a San Felipe dawn,
name him Salvador. They'll rest
    beneath a web spun umbilical,
eclipsed from our human eyes.

•

Our Lady

      stone   clay

            earth
                rain
                  orphaned
        heart

eclipsed

IYAWÓ

Soneto de Silueta

For Ana Mendieta

ud learns to live with mites, worms, beetles, and ticks.

nd Lioness digs up the earth where a warthog cowers in his den.

ou know you are loved when she tears you to bits, brittle thing.

The lioness tongue softens you up all the way to her bottom.

Roots, straw, weeds, rain your crown, *hija de Ochun*.

Even Earth's suffering arises from pangs of love.

When Lioness fangs diffuse the blood we call it liberation.

Wax hisses from the smoldering wick, curtains you draw go *shoosh*.

The last earth imprint you ever left on asphalt from thirty floors up.

A shoe curved from the work your instep leaves behind.

The breath of the lioness heats up your shoulders and your neck.

A genetic photograph of every cell that ever lives exists in a lioness
mouth.

She tears into the riverbed and root hairs clog her claws.

Ancient bacteria get all up in you.

Control the fire and it burns deeper, flashing life into sleeping
embers.

Man on Fire, 1969, by Luis Jiménez

Why Being "On Fire" Is for Everyone

Because the facial features burn fastest.

Because the sun sets in Tibet before it ever rises in the West.

Because Tsering Tashi's mother told him to dress in the thickest,
finest, llama wool *chuba*.

For I find no flattering explanation for the murder of everyone.

Flames consume the head, hands, and feet in the mural by Orozco.

Because monks don't even eat meat.

His clothes made him torch; still Thích Quảng Đức's heart would
not fire.

Because his remains stiffened when they tried to place him in a
tomb.

Because what is the point of murdering everyone in the world?

Since the sun sets in Vietnam before it reaches the West.

Because aren't the faceless Mexicans always the ones we martyr?

Why do heretic Indians hurry to incinerate themselves at the stake?

Are you awake enough to remember how we clarify the skin of our
slaves?

To feel the fingers of the children of thread flame stitching your
voluminous rugs?

The candles in the basilica flicker when they channel the nightmares
of the dead.

Because Jiménez wept when the mammoth blue mustang leg fell
from heaven, rupturing the artery in his leg.

Because of Chinese soldiers armed to protect Tiananmen Square
from monks burning to set themselves ablaze.

Luis says he's sorry for the pain he caused you having to finish his
stallion.

Larry Levan (snake), 2006, by Elia Alba

VALERIE MARTÍNEZ

Larry Levan (snake)

Hip hip hip hip hip makes the man
    as the conga, serpentine,
        slides across the frame

and the disco dub — tilt and sway —
    sewing pelves in the room,
        as if Larry, still,

were levitating streetwise
    Blacks, Drags, Latinos, Punks:
        Saturday Mass, 1985,

in the Paradise Garage — Evelyn
    "Champagne" King, Kraftwerk,
        Ashra.

No. He's black-and-white, a head shot,
    one two three
        four five,

on this S curve of 21st-century revelers,
    mask on the one body
        down,

shimmer slant of a hoop earring
    under the ten-leg-
        hop-and-pulsate —

glide on through. And Larry, Dour Father,
    bubble pop-popped,
        afloat,

asking repeatedly: *Who, My Friends,*
    is fronting? Who is not?
        You,

Velvet Valance, over the sequined
drag of curtain.
Black is Black,

Brown is Brown, Gay is Gay disco
pulsing up and through
seventeen years

of not-forbidding bodies. Introibo
ad altare Dei. Ad Deum
qui lætificat

juventutem meam. *Gather you*
to me and to one another.
Grind.

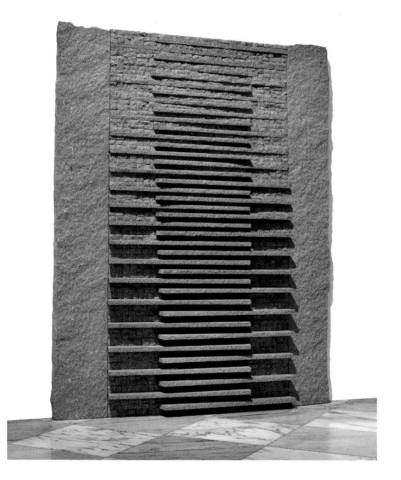

Granite Weaving, 1988, by Jesús Moroles

Granite Weaving

To climb, in this instance, upon a horizon

Shadow-shadow. Lip-to-lip rock.

Ziggurat. Ah, from the base to the top.

Sideways. Upwards. Again, in succession.

Sprung and sprung

Frozen idiom.

Barre. Pietrasanta. Mouth and mouth.

Sung. Granite. Stitching

The way fabric gathers — pinch, scrunch.

Not in dreams alone. Not the knot.

Step, step, step, step, step. 35 up.

As if into clouds

Ur, Aqar Quf, Chogha Zanbil, Tikal.

Kin.

Plank upon plank upon plank upon

Little Blocks: *ahem. don't you forget us.*

a, of, or, but, if, la, and

Close and closer to flattened.

Rock, Water, Bone: Noisy Pilgrim.

Weaving Granite

"He" grates across the throat, the "h" a dry abrasion on the tongue —
Across the throat, the "h" in "she" is tucked behind the folded
    muscle.
In "she" is tucked the "e" the lips unpurse to say, same as saying "we."
My lips unpurse to say the names of God, of Love, and they are "She."
The names of God, of Love are, too, old explosions coded into
    granite.
Too, old explosions cooled to stone warm to the touch of light, as she,
Stone-warmed and glowing, let my lips brush velvet shadows onto
    hers.
Let my lips brush the story soft, forget that "he" was scrape and
    struggle.
The story soft forgets that "he" was heavy, wrestled into "we," and
    weaving
"He" heavy, wrestled (strands of granite yarned like fabric) into "we,"
Strands of granite halt their dry abrasion, interlock, and become "She."

À La Mode, 1976, by Asco (photographer: Harry Gamboa, Jr.)

A Chingona Plays Miss Dinah Brand

I dare you to hear me
tell just which and what
sort of girl I was, always
had been, and why. You
may as well yes-yes me.
You'll get no chance to
cut in. This is No Movie
and I'm the leading gal,
the femme fatale in cork
platform sandals, mis-
taking Woolworth's
plastic earrings for
glam, mis-american,
which and what sort?
The kind who never
introduces the top six
buttons of her dress
to their holes, whose
legs always cross
when she sits on a
table, who pats vanilla
pancake over her rich,
theatrical skin to lift
dark hair, dark eyes, dark
lips from the level
of East Los Common
to revelation, and you're
all in my made-up
fairy tale now, you &
these suave muchachos,
we're all queasy in the
where is it 40s 50s 60s
70s brown beautiful
people pronouncing our perfect
English, accorded

zero-to-slivers of
silver screen glory.
I dare you, looking
in from the tangled
reel of the future,
say out loud what I'm
sitting on. Kitten-posed
on a table top in Philippe's
Original Sandwich Shop,
Los Angeles, '76, next
to the napkins and
sugar shaker, I'm not
afraid of the cleaning rag
wiping me out of the frame,
I take in the unedited
numbers that tumble
in one continuous shot
from my Now to yours,
and there's a mestiza
born every minute, I
know where I sit:
right on top of a
pretty warm piece
of sweet American pie.

Untitled, 1965, by Alberto Valdés

TINO VILLANUEVA

Field of Moving Colors Layered

I'm not easily mesmerized.
But how can you not be drawn in by swirls,
angles and whorls brought together to obey
a field of moving colors layered, muted ...
others bright that make you linger
there?
Just look at those Carpaccio reds.

Right then my mind
leaps to Cezanne:
his dark-blue vest in *Self-Portrait* (1879–1880);
the *Seven Bathers* (ca. 1900) wallowing in blue;
his blue beyond in *Château Noir* (1904).

Consider now the three, or is it four figures
in Alberto Valdés's *Untitled* (ca. 1965).
They are wayward energy, moving right
to left (the right one more sensuous than the rest)
about to dive
into the deep-blue waiting — call it the unknown.
I'd like to be there when they meet that blue abyss
head on.
Will they keep their shape, I wonder,
or break up and rearrange themselves
into a brighter, more memorable pose
... into a bigger elemental thing?

I'm really asking this:
When they run into the landscape of blue,
will these figures lose their logic of luster?
Will they lose their lucid argument of color,
their accumulated wealth of geometry?
Will they still engage the entire me,
hold me,
keep me mesmerized?

Humane Borders Water Station, 2004, by Delilah Montoya

EDUARDO C. CORRAL

Testament Scratched into a Water Station Barrel
(Translation #11)

Far from highways I flicker
    gold the whispering
        gasoline
if I pinch her nipples
    too hard
        no joy for her
no joy for me
    so I practice on ticks
        press them
just so so they give
    but do not burst
        beneath
my boots
    thistle & puncture vine
    a wild horse
asleep on all fours
    its shadow still grazing
        my lips
black meat
    my tongue
    black meat
in my backpack
    sardine tins
        saltines
& a few cough drops
    the moon is my library
        there's a glacier
inside a grain of salt
    do you understand
        I'm sorry
my Albanian
    isn't very good
        tremble
if God forgets you

tremble
                if God
remembers you
        out of clay I shape
                        sparrows
I glaze their bills & claws
        I give them names
                        like gossamer
inglenook lagoon
        she bathed
                a trumpet
in milk
        her tenderness acoustic
                        & plural
her pupils perched
        in all that green
                there's nudity
around the corner
        bones cracked
                        & iridescent
sometimes it rains so hard
        even the moon
                        puts on
a raincoat
        zinc razz zinc jazz
                I notch my arms
I notch my thighs
        five six days
                I score
my skin but not
        the back of my knees
                        two ovals
two portraits
        my son at ten
                his eyes ablaze

my son at one
      his eyes shut
            once
I dressed him in burlap
      once bicycles
         & marbles
once I tore rain
      out of a parable
         to strike down
his thirst

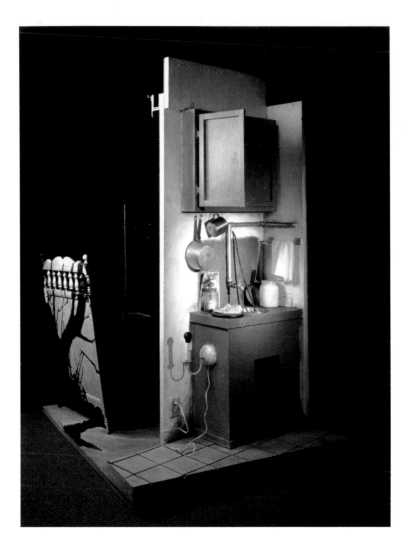

El Patio de Mi Casa, 1990, by María Brito

ORLANDO RICARDO MENES

El Patio de Mi Casa

My patio was once a schoolyard, or maybe a barracoon, perhaps both, & the ghosts of children nest under the pink sink, mouths agape for flakes of rust, or they creep to the ceiling, sucking on the five taps of blue water, their little lips abuzz like cicadas. In the moonlight I see them bounce on my feather bed, bowed like an old donkey's back, or they teeter-totter in my wicker chair darned with burlap string. Leave them alone, I say to my mother, who wants to cleanse the house with carvacrol, trapping these children's souls in beehives, then stringing them up with kites so they fly to the moon. Let them drum our dented pots, let them screech happy carols, let them dance with tin spurs on their little feet. Mother, I don't care if they nibble our family photos, soil your heirlooms of lace, or steal what few grains of rice (more like gypsum ants) you hoard in the pink pantry. Let them play cat's cradle with spiderwebs, let them rummage in your armoire of moths, let them lurk in your shadows of ill will & tease you to laughter. Ghosts are unruly, free to be fickle, unlike me, the pig-tailed girl you kept strapped to the sewing machine in the shed of planks by the mango tree too old to fruit. Work & sweat will set you free, you said, just like Fidel on the radio. Cut me out of those sepia photos on the wall, burn those baby braids you keep in porcelain, toss my first communion gown into the sea. I wish I'd been born into a brood of mice, quick to grow, quick to breed, quick to die among the kapok trees.

Sin Título, from the series *The Tempest*, 1998, by Arturo Rodríguez

Altar Boy

I am the altar boy with feet flattened by the catechist's paddle, my skin toasted like stalks of sugarcane at Lent, my shorts baptized in the salt pans of saints. I don't wear a mask (God hates carnival) but a wool hood, Holy Week's, that Sister Rose knitted by the charcoal altar, her wooden teeth clacking as she hymned in Latin, the moles on her jowl like prickly pears for penance. My own teeth are those grates that grilled the martyrs, & my little lamb's ears quiver each afternoon when the wind coughs in fits and pale skies smoke with incense from a clandestine Mass, perhaps on a runaway shallop with sails sewn from stolen cassocks, perhaps on a newborn isle with a thatched church, novices crawling like iguanas around stations of the cross. There's no home for orphans like us raised in a convent by the wharf where the footless angel blows his trumpet for vesper, and the abbess marches us to the clapboard altar when the cock crows. We sleep in straw cubbies, our sheets those crinkled newspapers that swaddled us like groupers in the foundling's basket. Hey, you, girl with the twisted neck, your dollhouse will keep on shrinking between your dirty legs. Not even holy water can make you clean. Hey, boy, the more you pull on the kite, the more your house of dreams will get lost in summer's wayward clouds. Let us live in the meadow, our true home, every bush a hearth, every pond a font: O blessed loam of nettles whose fireflies light the shrine at night, whose blue brooks spread out like veins of Calvary.

Decoy Gang War Victim, 1974, by Asco (photographer: Harry Gamboa, Jr.)

Decoy Gang War Victim

For Harry Gamboa, Jr.

Just a tick ago, the actor was a Roman candle
shot to the sky, smudged by rain's helter-
skelter. His motivation was: he's a stooge
on L.A.'s sodden turnpike, so we have "to make" art. Got
to rezone and react. The world the bare wall to
his bullet. Got to rile up the populace, to fortify
the arsenal. Once in a while, repopulate and penetrate,
paint a list of incitement onto the walls.
An elder told him that to overturn the city, one must
surrender body/belongings to the one explosive
spectacle of truth, making it ongoing. Pay attention.
To overturn the city, not just the scraps but fervor itself.
Not just the wan broadcast of indignation but
IRL incursions into the workhouses and
poorhouses to inflame the thousand points of light.
A lean surge, departure pinks both ends of him.
He's the nth layer folded into the stand's nerve.

¿Sólo una sombra?/Only a Shadow (Ester IV)?, from the series *Santos y sombras/ Saints and Shadows*, 1993–1994, by Muriel Hasbun

Only a Shadow

My daughter gathers the seeds she finds in our desert, calls them
spirits — *the spirits are us*, she says when I worry those orbs in my
    fingers

to conjure her birth. The wind's first thought is to craft those seeds:
vessels when the tree worries she's not enough of a multiplicity,

that she will burn into the cosmos. The cosmos is no thought, no
    worry,
more than us, but less than wind, and the wind is only the infinite,

not the body's death, which is, after all, only a particle, but time
    formless
as space. This is only if the wind worries at all. The seed doesn't
    think

— she is the doubling ambition of a vessel. In the wind, the idea
of the copy is translated by time. We were once that idea. My
    daughter

collects me in a box marked for spirits where I unsettle the other
    seeds
begging for wind so that my sound will echo a thousand miles away.

My daughter was the pulse I toss into the wind with the seeds.
    Particles
of us pass over like whispers from the cosmos, the clatter

the wind makes. I worry birds will take her into themselves,
that she'll become a fleck of their transience, but this is how we
    furrow

ourselves into the cosmos, the twine of our breaths into wind, into
carbon, into the tree's colossal fingers reaching back from under the
    earth.

Humanscape 62, 1970, by Melesio Casas

LAURIE ANN GUERRERO

Brownies of the Southwest: Troop 704

Three years before I'd hear the word / *beaner* /
from the / white boys / who'd spit first in my broccoli,
then in my hair, / my mother / dressed me

each Wednesday in that / brown / sheath: I was seven.
It'd be the only time I'd wear a sash —
Miss / America, / she said.

Twenty Miss / Americas, we made /
kitsch from clothespins, pipe cleaners —
our / brown / socks / banded and complicated /

with orange tassels just below the / brown /
/ rosettes / of our knees, little / skulls / knocking
together in our elementary / school / cafeteria.

How we jumped the day / we heard / voices
raising there instead of / at home, / when Tracy's
mom slapped our / troop / leader / and Tracy

cried. And Tracy's / mom was white /
and only her / dad was brown / and Tracy
was a little / prettier than the rest of us. /

At the lunch tables, / *white bitch* / stuck to our fingers
like glue; / *fucking Mexicans* / landed like glitter
onto the sashes laid across our / small / hearts. /

With Tracy, / we watched / manifest between us
/ a line, / risen from the tiled floor where / we shared /
meals as tears clung to the eye-rims of my seven-year-old

/ compañeras. / Lorena chewed her nails till blood
/ bloomed / on her ring finger. Andrea peed quietly
/ on her brown knee / socks. None of us knew

where to hide. This was not / home, /
where / we could run / to the / broom / closet
or to the / feet / of our big / brothers. /

Breakfast Tacos, from the series *Seven Days*, 2003, by Chuck Ramirez

Last Meal: Breakfast Tacos, San Antonio, Tejas

Let me be your last meal.
Let me harvest the notes
I took from your mother's
watery hands, street vendors
in Rome, Ms. Rosie
from our taquería, you:
in the sun, in the open air,
let me give you zucchini
and their elusive blossoms —
my arms, my hands.
Pumpkiny empanadas
of my feet, pulpy as a newborn's.
Guisada'd loin of my calf
muscle. On a plate white
and crisp as the ocean,
lemoned eyeballs like two
scallops. The red, ripe
plum of my mouth.
Perhaps with coffee,
you'd have the little lobe
of my ear sugared as a wedding
cookie. The skin of my belly,
my best chicharrón, scrambled
with the egg of my brain
for your breakfast tacos.
My lengua like lengua.
Mi pescuezo, el mejor hueso.
Let me be your last meal:
mouthfuls of my never-to-be-digested
face, my immovable femur
caught in your throat
like a fish bone. Let my body be
what could never leave your body.

Acknowledgements

All images courtesy of and with permission from the Smithsonian American Art Museum. *Night Magic (Blue Jester)* by Carlos Almaraz, gift of Gloria Werner © 1988, Carlos Almaraz Estate. *Nocturnal (Horizon Line)* by Teresita Fernández, museum purchase through the Luisita L. and Franz H. Denghausen Endowment © 2010, Teresita Fernández. *Platanal* by Myrna Báez, gift of Jaime Fonalledas. *Radiante* by Olga Albizu, gift of JPMorgan Chase. *Placa/Rollcall* by Charles "Chaz" Bojórquez, gift of the artist. *Untitled*, from the *Silueta* series by Ana Mendieta, museum purchase through the Smithsonian Latino Initiatives Pool and the Smithsonian Institution Collections Acquisition Program © 1980, Estate of Ana Mendieta. *Man on Fire* by Luis Jiménez, gift of Philip Morris Incorporated © 1969, Luis Jiménez. *Larry Levan (snake)* by Elia Alba, museum purchase made possible by William W.W. Parker © 2006, Elia Alba. *Granite Weaving* by Jesús Moroles, gift of Frank K. Ribelin. *À La Mode* by Asco (photographer: Harry Gamboa, Jr.), museum purchase through the Luisita L. and Franz H. Denghausen Endowment © 1976, Harry Gamboa, Jr. *Untitled* by Alberto Valdés, gift of David and Susan Valdés. *Humane Borders Water Station* by Delilah Montoya, gift of the Gilberto Cárdenas Latino Art Collection © 2004, Delilah Montoya. *El Patio de Mi Casa* by María Brito, museum purchase through the Smithsonian Institution Collections Acquisition Program © 1991, María Brito. *Sin Título*, from the series *The Tempest* by Arturo Rodríguez, gift of Liza and Pedro J. Martinez-Fraga. *Decoy Gang War Victim* by Asco (photographer: Harry Gamboa, Jr.), museum purchase through the Luisita L. and Franz H. Denghausen Endowment © 1974, Harry Gamboa, Jr. *¿Sólo una sombra?/Only a Shadow (Ester IV)?*, from the series *Santos y sombras/Saints and Shadows* by Muriel Hasbun, gift of Mr. and Mrs. Charles H. Moore © 1994, Muriel Hasbun. *Humanscape 62* by Melesio Casas, museum purchase through the Luisita L. and Franz H. Denghausen Endowment © 1970, the Casas Family. *Breakfast Tacos*, from the series *Seven Days* by Chuck Ramirez, museum purchase through the Luisita L. and Franz H. Denghausen Endowment © 2003, Estate of Charles Ramirez.

COMMENT

CHRISTINA PUGH

On Ghosts and the Overplus

Tonight I saw myself in the dark window as
the image of my father, whose life
was spent like this,
thinking of death, to the exclusion
of other sensual matters,
so in the end that life
was easy to give up, since
it contained nothing.
— From *Mirror Image*, by Louise Glück

You can spend your whole life thinking of death. Or soaring from it. My father was the opposite of Glück's — steeped instead in the earthly, the decimal point, and the profit margin. Eight years into leukemia and he still had no time for death — no truck with it, as people used to say. He was a retired businessman still chairing company committees. He was a master gardener, devising ever new systems for labeling squash and trellising tomatoes. He was industrious, in the best sense. Frost might have said that his vocation and avocation had successfully united, as two eyes do in sight. Hospice was the roadblock. His own mortality was the real shock.

Hospice broke his heart.

This is the story I'm telling right now. I believe it to be true. Or might there have been another, different truth — some truth beyond a living person's need to understand? I'd like to imagine a veiled waterway, hidden even from himself, that led him to a place beyond his conscious will and power. Could some internal stream have soothed the pain of his body's betrayal? I'm guaranteed never to know. But I can still wish.

Can poetry reside in the recess of that mystery?

•

There used to be no house, hardly a room, in which someone had not once died.
— From *Illuminations*, by Walter Benjamin

Some years ago, a friend was talking to an owl at an artists' colony near the Bighorns. Every morning before sunrise, she went out to greet the owl, and the owl spoke back. I understood that some profound content had been exchanged between the two of them — though it was also, perhaps predictably, hard to pin down in English. So I didn't press her too hard for details.

What stayed with me instead was the euphoria of *address* — what Roman Jakobson called the conative function in language, or "orientation toward the addressee." I like to think of it this way: the conversation's subject isn't really so important; the thrill is that the conversation happens at all. The linguistic rush of *face to face*. Or in French, conversation is *tête à tête*: literally "head to head," or putting two heads together.

This is what it feels like to fall in love.

Still, wouldn't you be skeptical about the owl story?

A few years later, during my own stay at a colony, I myself became the surprised target of a "visitation" — a ghost. It was said that a person, or persons, had died in the house where I was staying. One of them followed me up the staircase and spoke in my dark bedroom. Tripped the electrical circuit's "light fantastic." And made my keyboarding fingers type the initials "BS" — in a succinct (and, yes, hilarious) pan of everything I'd written that day.

The other residents there didn't find my experience unusual. They had their own, similar stories. One of them told me not to worry.

To me, it had felt terrifying and then a little silly. A good agnostic, and a good empiricist, is not supposed to be visited like this, even if she's also a poet. I couldn't square that ghost — but I couldn't deny its existence, either. It had all really happened. So I tried to redefine it as a local artifact. Or put it in the zoo. I told myself, *Ghosts are part of the discourse here*.

That sentence is a paradox: *discourse* sparks the intellect while *ghost* flouts its every rule. The sentence is also a diplomat — it brings reason and inexplicability to the same table. Most of all, though, it muzzles the ghost. *Discourse* routs the uncontainable. The uncountable. I fenced that ghost in language.

Since poetry is made of words—as Mallarmé told Degas—it's capable of doing this, too. But a poem is also something else. Poetry is what lets the ghost reply, *Don't fence me in.*

•

> You have told me you gave it all away
> then, sold the house, keeping only the confirmation
> cross she wore, her name in cursive chased
> on the gold underside, your ring in the same
>
> box, those photographs you still avoid,
> and the quilt you spread on your borrowed bed—
> small things. Months after we met, you told me she had
> made it, after we had slept already beneath its loft
> and thinning, raveled pattern, as though beneath
> her shadow, moving with us, that dark, that soft.
>   — From *Artifact*, by Claudia Emerson

Look at the smallest, most ephemeral things around you. How many fingers have touched them? Do you know whose?

In Claudia Emerson's sequence "Late Wife: Letters to Kent," a newly remarried woman encounters her husband's first wife, dead of cancer, in precisely those sorts of things. There is the quilt the late wife made, and one stray "driving glove" in the car. The late wife also made a video of her then-husband Kent coming home to their adorably excitable dog.

When she watches this home video, Emerson realizes that its erstwhile camerawoman and "director" is now, impossibly, directing *her*: "as though she directs/me to notice the motion of her chest/in the rise and fall of the frame." Kent—the "you" in this passage from "Homecoming"—is unwittingly complicit in the strategy:

> Then, at last, you come home
> to look into the camera she holds,
> and past her into me—invisible, unimagined
> other who joins her in seeing through our
> transience the lasting of desire.

The "you," the "me," and the "she." Three pronouns that don't always go well together. But this particular triangle is full of generosity. Emerson becomes the late wife's coconspirator, confidante, receptor, continuation. Kent is the natural bridge: love for him has brought two strangers together, one posthumously, in these poems' "unimagined" scenes. A single wife is not enough; two marriages combine in time to serve an idea, or "the lasting of desire."

I don't know how "true" these poems are, nor do I need to know. In other words, I don't know whether, or to what degree, Emerson actually experienced the late wife as I did the ghost at the colony. Regardless, I see her poems as an act of radical empathy and eros — one that reimagined and loosened the outlines of a single self, or of a couple. It was an act that redefined triangulation not as tension or obstacle — the way it has been since time immemorial, or at least since *Jane Eyre* — but as the perfecting of each couple's love, moving forward and backward in time.

I didn't know Claudia Emerson. She died in 2014, also from cancer, at the young age of fifty-seven. When I read the news, my mind flew to *Late Wife*. It was all I could think about. At first, I felt it all had to be a mistake: that *Late Wife* made Emerson's early death impossible. As if the book itself should have been a prophylactic. Then I wondered if the opposite were true.

I wondered, that is, if the poems were talismanic. They didn't foretell Emerson's death, but they narrated what had, in a sense, already happened: she herself was in the process of becoming the "late wife" that the poems so lovingly inhabited.

In a sense, every poem becomes a site of *askesis*, or self-evacuation — since we don't write literally with blood, but with black marks on paper, or their electronic equivalents. As we learn in our first workshops, our bodies (and explanations, and justifications) can't follow our poems around in the world. But Emerson's askesis seems different, as if she exchanged her very life for a rapt concentration on the dead. The danger of that statement, of course, is that it sounds a lot like magical thinking. It sounds like an aesthetic justification for a death that occurred too soon.

And maybe it is. But consider this: elsewhere in the poem I just quoted, Emerson calls the late wife's video "scripted." In the course of writing these poems, had Emerson tapped into something more powerful than poetry, or even than her life? In this case, the rhetorical term is *prolepsis* — meaning that, in some sense, we are always living with a future that has already happened.

What role can poetry play in such a life-script? Here are the first wife's X-rays, as her doctors described them to Kent:

> By the time they saw what they were looking at
> it was already risen into the bones
> of her chest. They could show you then the lungs
> were white with it; they said it was like salt
> in water — that hard to see as separate —
> and would be that hard to remove. Like moonlight
> dissolved in fog, in the dense web
> of vessels.
>
> — From *The X-Rays*

Like the disease in the lungs, metaphor is everywhere. It's ineluctable, even in the doctors' diagnosis. The first wife's illness becomes beautiful as an ocean or as moonlight dissolved in fog. It seems to me there is always a risk in lyricizing pathology, but I also sense that this is the perfect accommodation — the hand-in-driving-glove, if you will — between the ghost of the late wife and the poet who will become her successor. Like salt in water, the two of them had already grown so very hard to see as separate.

Maybe metaphor incites such eerie inevitability, which became the achievement of Emerson's Pulitzer Prize-winning book. Yet the poet's biography shows that the poems themselves are not the end. It calls us beyond the poems, into the script.

This is what made Emerson's death the hardest-hitting for me, despite our recent and staggering losses of giants like Seamus Heaney, Philip Levine, and Mark Strand. Strand who, in one of his last talks at the Poetry Foundation, discussed "the inevitability of surprise" in poems. He said that current poetry fashion had lost the taste for it.

Though she was alive when he spoke it, Strand's phrase also describes Emerson's demise.

•

> All I know is a door into the dark.
> — From *The Forge*, by Seamus Heaney

The history of the novel has a discrete historical place for the Gothic and its revenants. In poetry, though, the ghost can't be confined to a single era. Claudia Emerson had so many ancestors. There was Coleridge and "Christabel." Hardy's final ghost poems. Rilke "transcribing" the sonnets to Orpheus, inspired by the dead Vera Knoop. Yeats writing *A Vision*. Merrill and his Ouija board. And so on.

Why do so many of these ghosts seep into the lives and deaths of poets? All I know is that the more I write poetry, the surer and less sure I become. The more deeply I listen to both the inflections and innuendoes of language, to paraphrase Wallace Stevens, the more astute and also superstitious I seem to be. The more densely I describe the textures of the world around me, the more of it I realize I am missing. The negatives of Matthew Brady's Civil War photographs, built into greenhouse glass and described by Linda Bierds in *The Profile Makers*, make lovely analogues for this. Of course, it's a short journey from photographic negatives to Keatsian negative capability, or the valuation of doubt and mystery that animates so many poets.

For me, poetry proliferates and flourishes in the intellect's blind spot. But you have to have the intellect first; you can't skip that step. I find intelligence to be most interesting when it's tested — not when it's challenged, but when we restrain it from being the default mode by which we apprehend the phenomena around us. Can strategies in the martial arts speak to this?

By the same token, the way of mind that attends the supernatural or numinous is hardly compelling without a formidable and even mutually exclusive foil. Ratiocination. This is where poetry inserts itself, again with Stevens, as what "must resist the intelligence / Almost successfully."

•

My Ben!
Or come again,
Or send to us
Thy wit's great overplus.
     — From *An Ode to Ben Jonson*, by Robert Herrick

The dead have no ears, no answering machines
that we know of, still we call.
     — From *Leave a Message*, by Bob Hicok

The "O" of apostrophe. The vocative, in Latin — and for Jakobson, too. For the critic Barbara Johnson, apostrophe was what made lyric poetry itself; its long history could have been distilled into a single cry. Robert Herrick's apostrophe transformed his dead friend, the bon vivant Ben Jonson, into "Saint Ben." We cry to the dead, and we imagine that they answer us. The weirdness in me wants to say they sometimes even do.

Herrick was right, too, about the dead's "overplus." This is the uncanny excess that can't be contained by empirical limits — even if it's sheathed in Jonson's wit or my own ghost's "BS." If Herrick's term sounds mathematical, so much the better. Think of the late wife's doctors and their metaphors.

Can we greet overplus without relinquishing our skepticism? Poetry keeps asking the impossible.

My father died two years ago today, in my childhood home that had become, for six short and endless hours, Hospice. His pain ripped him, even with morphine. To the end, I think, he was battling death, his legs still muscled enough to fight.

When it was over, the funeral home attendants zipped up his body and wheeled it away, leaving a silk rose behind.

Later that night, I startled awake and sat up. He was lying next to me, as if still in his hospital bed. But his eyes were peacefully closed, the way they hadn't been in death. His face and body were calm — as if conflict and even muscularity had flown, or floated down a river. I leaned over and reached for his hand, then realized I was clawing my own bedsheet.

He was there. Or not. How would I ever know?

In poetry, perhaps more than anywhere else, we can try.

The answers won't be there. Still we call.

FRANCISCO ARAGÓN* is the author of *Glow of Our Sweat* (Scapegoat Press, 2010). He teaches at the University of Notre Dame and directs Letras Latinas.

JOHN ASHBERY's latest collection of poems is *Breezeway* (Ecco, 2015); a two-volume set of his collected translations from the French, edited by Rosanne Wasserman and Eugene Richie, was published in 2014 (Farrar, Straus and Giroux).

DENISE BERGMAN* is, most recently, the author of the poetry books *A Woman in Pieces Crossed a Sea* (West End Press, 2014) and *The Telling* (Červená Barva Press, 2014).

FELIX BERNSTEIN* is the author of *Burn Book* (Nightboat Books, 2016), and *Notes on Post-Conceptual Poetry* (Insert Blanc Press, 2015).

CACONRAD's latest book is *ECODEVIANCE: (Soma)tics for the Future Wilderness* (Wave Books, 2014).

BRENDA CÁRDENAS* is the author of *Boomerang* (Bilingual Press/Editorial Bilingüe, 2009). She teaches at the University of Wisconsin–Milwaukee and was Milwaukee's Poet Laureate from 2010–2012.

LORNA DEE CERVANTES's* most recent book is *Sueño: New Poems* (Wings Press, 2013).

EDUARDO C. CORRAL is the author of *Slow Lightning* (Yale University Press, 2012). He teaches in the low-residency MFA program at Pacific University.

KWAME DAWES's* forthcoming collection of poems is *City of Bones* (Northwestern University Press). He is Glenna Luschei Editor of *Prairie Schooner* at the University of Nebraska–Lincoln.

BLAS FALCONER* is the author of *The Foundling Wheel* (Four Way Books, 2012) and *A Question of Gravity and Light* (University of Arizona Press, 2007).

ALEC FINLAY's* recent books include *I Hear Her Cry* (Ingleby Gallery, 2015) and *Global Oracle* (Morning Star, 2014). "Billia Croo" was first published in *ebban an' flowan*, by Alec Finlay and Dr. Laura

Watts, with photographs by Alistair Peebles (Morning Star, 2015).

LAURIE ANN GUERRERO* is the Texas Poet Laureate and is the author of *A Crown for Gumecindo* (Aztlan Libre Press, 2015) and *A Tongue in the Mouth of the Dying* (University of Notre Dame Press, 2013).

REBECCA HAZELTON is the author of *Vow* (Cleveland State University Poetry Center, 2013) and *Fair Copy* (Ohio State University Press, 2012).

JUAN FELIPE HERRERA* is the Poet Laureate of the United States. His poem in this issue is copyright © 2015 by Juan Felipe Herrera. Reprinted by permission of City Lights Books.

IYAWÓ (Kristin Naca) is the author of *Bird Eating Bird* (Harper Perennial, 2009). Her poems and essay, "Life Altars," detailing her initiation as a santera, appear in *Art Papers*.

MARIA MELENDEZ KELSON published *Flexible Bones* (2010) and *How Long She'll Last in This World* (2006) with University of Arizona Press. She teaches at Pueblo Community College in Colorado.

GRETCHEN MARQUETTE's* first book, *May Day*, is forthcoming from Graywolf Press in 2016. She lives in Minneapolis.

VALERIE MARTÍNEZ* is the author of four books of poetry, including *Each and Her* (University of Arizona Press, 2010) and *Absence, Luminescent* (Four Way Books, 1999).

ORLANDO RICARDO MENES* is professor of English in the Creative Writing Program at the University of Notre Dame. His fifth poetry collection is *Heresies* (University of New Mexico Press, 2015).

DANTE MICHEAUX* is the author of *Amorous Shepherd* (Sheep Meadow Press, 2010). He resides in London.

CARL PHILLIPS's most recent book of poems is *Reconnaissance* (Farrar, Straus and Giroux, 2015).

CHRISTINA PUGH's recent books are *Grains of the Voice* (TriQuarterly Books, 2013) and the forthcoming collection *Perception* (Four Way Books, 2017).

JAMES REIDEL* is the author of *Jim's Book* (2013) and *My Window Seat for Arlena Twigg* (2006) both from Black Lawrence Press. He is the biographer of Weldon Kees.

TOM SLEIGH's most recent book of poems is *Station Zed* (Graywolf Press, 2015).

CARMEN GIMÉNEZ SMITH is the author of a memoir and four poetry collections including *Milk and Filth* (University of Arizona Press, 2013). She is the editor-in-chief of *Puerto del Sol*.

LEAH UMANSKY is the author of *Straight Away the Emptied World* (forthcoming) and *Don Dreams and I Dream* (2014), both from Kattywompus Press.

TINO VILLANUEVA* is the author of seven books of poetry, including *So Spoke Penelope* (Grolier Poetry Press, 2013) and *Scene from the Movie GIANT* (Curbstone Press, 1993).

JEFF ZIMMERMANN* has exhibited large scale murals internationally. His work has been featured on *TODAY* and in the *New York Times*.

* First appearance in *Poetry*.

Sewanee Writers' Conference

WORKSHOPS IN POETRY, FICTION, AND PLAYWRITING
JULY 19–31, 2016

THE UNIVERSITY OF THE SOUTH SEWANEE, TENNESSEE

Accepting applications through April 15
Thanks to the generosity of the Walter E. Dakin Memorial Fund, supported by the estate of Tennessee Williams, every participant receives assistance covering two-thirds of the actual cost to attend. Additional funding is awarded to fellows and scholars.

FACULTY & READERS
Daniel Anderson
Richard Bausch
John Casey
Tony Earley
B.H. Fairchild
Adrianne Harun
Robert Hass
Andrew Hudgins
Naomi Iizuka
Mark Jarman
Randall Kenan
Maurice Manning
Charles Martin
Jill McCorkle
Alice McDermott
Erin McGraw
Marilyn Nelson
Dan O'Brien
Wyatt Prunty
Christine Schutt
A.E. Stallings
Sidney Wade
Allen Wier
Steve Yarbrough

VISITORS & LECTURERS
Millicent Bennett
Beth Blickers
Paul Bone
Valerie Borchardt
Michelle Brower
Sarah Burnes
MaryKatherine
   Callaway
George David
   Clark
Barbara Epler
Gary Fisketjon
Mary Flinn
Emily Forland
Rob Griffith
Gail Hochman
Mike Levine
David Lynn
Speer Morgan
Kathy Pories
Elisabeth Schmitz
Anna Stein
Philip Terzian
N.S. Thompson
Liz Van Hoose
Les Waters
Michael Wiegers
Amy Williams
Robert Wilson
David Yezzi
Renée Zuckerbrot

931.598.1654 | swc@sewanee.edu
sewaneewriters.org

Phillis Levin
MR. MEMORY
& Other Poems
Levin's fifth collection of poems encompasses a wide array of styles and voices while staying true to a visionary impulse sparked as much by the smallest detail as the most sublime landscape.
Penguin Poets • 96 pages • 978-0-14-312811-3 • $18.00

Amy Gerstler
SCATTERED AT SEA
A dazzling new collection—long-listed for the 2015 National Book Award for Poetry. "This wry book is like a wave that knocks you over and changes how you view the world.... [It] mixes salty humor, invigorating rhythms and sharp-edged wisdom." —*The Washington Post.*
Penguin Poets • 96 pages • 978-0-14-312689-8 • $20.00

Lia Purpura
IT SHOULDN'T
HAVE BEEN BEAUTIFUL
"Purpura zooms in to scrutinize the bittersweet pivot that takes place in us when the world does not meet our desires. These poems are rooted in wonder, in the wide, dislocating pressures of mystery."—Joanna Klink.
Penguin Poets • 112 pages • 978-0-14-312690-4 • $20.00

Sarah Vap
VIABILITY
A winner of the National Poetry Series, *Viability* is an ambitious and highly imaginative collection of prose poems that braids together several kinds of language strands in an effort to understand and to ask questions about the bodies (and minds, maybe even souls) that are owned by capitalism. "This polyphonic assemblage brilliantly collapses the gap between lyric poetry and life." —Mary Jo Bang.
Penguin Poets • 176 pages • 978-0-14-312828-1 • $22.00

Mary Oliver
FELICITY
The Pulitzer prize-winning poet celebrates love in her latest collection. "One of the astonishing aspects of Oliver's work is the consistency of tone over [her career]. What changes is an increased focus on nature and an increased precision with language that has made her one of our very best poets."—Stephen Dobyns, *The New York Times Book Review.*
Penguin Press • 96 pages • 978-1-59420-676-4 • $24.95

Robert Morgan
DARK ENERGY
The award-winning poet's newest collection explores the mysteries and tensions of family and childhood, the splendors and hidden dramas of the natural world, and the agriculture that supports all culture.
Penguin Poets • 96 pages • 978-0-14-312806-9 • $18.00

Robyn Schiff
A WOMAN OF PROPERTY
"This brilliant revelation of having had and being winds like a spiral staircase down from the bedroom, into the garden, through violence and lust and contagion, to the Greek tragedy that is the foundation on which our American tragedy is built."—Eula Biss.
Penguin Poets • 96 pages • 978-0-14-312827-4 • $20.00

March Features

Poetry Podcasts | On the *Poetry* Magazine Podcast, *Poetry* editors **Don Share** and **Lindsay Garbutt** go inside the pages of this issue, talking to contributors and sharing their poem selections with listeners.

Poetry Off the Shelf, a bi-weekly podcast, explores the diverse world of contemporary American poetry.

Podcasts are available free from the iTunes store.

Harriet News | March's featured blogger, **Uche Nduka,** discusses poetry and poetics and life and politics in America, Nigeria and Germany at poetryfoundation.org/harriet

Learning Lab | View educational resources including poem guides to **Stevie Smith's "Not Waving but Drowning"** and **Walt Whitman's "Time to Come."**

Events | Plan your trip to the Poetry Foundation in Chicago to see some of our March events!

Poetry & Art
Jim Dine Reading & Presentation
Wednesday, March 9, 7:00 PM

Reading & Conversation
Amber Tamblyn with Hannah Gamble
Wednesday, March 16, 7:00 PM

Reading
Eiléan Ní Chuilleanáin, Conor O'Callaghan & Caitríona O'Reilly
Tuesday, March 29, 7:00 PM

Exhibition | **Bernadette Mayer: *Memory***
A poetic audio-visual installation from 1972
March 2016
Monday–Friday, 11:00 AM–4:00 PM

POETRY FOUNDATION
61 West Superior Street, Chicago, IL
(312) 787-7070

www.poetryfoundation.org